The Mysteries of
GOD

The Mysteries of
GOD

by
Maurice Roberts

REFORMATION HERITAGE BOOKS
Grand Rapids, Michigan

The Mysteries of God
© 2012 by Maurice Roberts

Reformation Heritage Books
2965 Leonard St. NE
Grand Rapids, MI 49525
616-977-0889 / Fax: 616-285-3246
orders@heritagebooks.org
www.heritagebooks.org

Printed in the United States of America
12 13 14 15 16 17/10 9 8 7 6 5 4 3 2 1

Library of Congress Cataloging-in-Publication Data

Roberts, Maurice.
  The mysteries of God / Maurice Roberts.
      p. cm.
   ISBN 978-1-60178-174-1 (pbk. : alk. paper)   1.   Bible. N.T.—
Theology. I. Title.
  BS2397.R63 2012
  230'.0415—dc23

                                   2012008125

For additional Reformed literature, request a free book list from Reformation Heritage Books at the above regular or e-mail address.

*Affectionately dedicated
to our daughter,*
Mary,

her husband,
John,

and their children,
Jonathan *and* **Joanna**

Table of Contents

Acknowledgments ix

1. What Is a New Testament Mystery? 1
2. The Mystery of God. 5
3. The Mystery of God's Covenant. 13
4. The Mystery of Godliness. 21
5. The Mystery of the Gospel 27
6. The Mystery of the New Birth 35
7. The Mystery of Christ's Glorious Indwelling 43
8. The Mystery of the Gospel Offer 49
9. The Mystery of the Gentiles. 57
10. The Mystery of Israel 67
11. The Mystery of Iniquity. 75
12. The Mystery of the Last Things 83
13. The Mystery of the Resurrection 91
14. When All Mysteries Are Finished 97

Acknowledgments

The author would like to express his gratitude to the following esteemed Christian friends: to the Rev. Sherman Isbell for valued assistance in the definition of the Holy Trinity in these pages and also to Pam Bateman, Susan Wallace, and Pamela Bugden for help over the years with typing sermons, articles, and lectures.

What Is a New Testament Mystery?

But we speak the wisdom of God in a mystery.
—1 CORINTHIANS 2:7

The word *mystery*, when used in the New Testament, is a technical term. It refers to an important truth that God has revealed to us in the Bible and that could not be known by the unaided mind of man. To be sure, there are some points of truth that man is able to deduce from the general revelation contained in the universe all around us. From looking at the heavens and the earth man can and ought to conclude that the world is created and designed by a great and powerful being—God.

Not all of our knowledge comes into the category of mystery. Some things we know by natural instinct and by our God-given conscience. Because we all have a conscience that provides an awareness of good and evil, it is our duty to differentiate between right and wrong. When we do what is wrong our conscience tells us that we are guilty and ought to be afraid of God. Even heathen societies with no access to the Bible have an understanding—although very defective and inadequate—of our need to have penalties for breaking the law.

However, there are many vital truths given to us in the Bible which, because it is God's revelation, give us a vastly greater understanding of God—His laws, His purposes, and His love—than the most intelligent heathen without a Bible could ever come to know. Such truths we refer to as mysteries, not because man has invented this term, but because it is the precise word that God Himself has chosen to inform us of His own wonderful way of salvation.

The apostle Paul explains the Bible's mysteries in this way: "Eye hath not seen, nor ear heard, neither have entered into the heart of man, the things which God hath prepared for them that love him" (1 Cor. 2:9). This is why the apostles were inspired by God to write their epistles in the New Testament. It was to tell us what the intelligent men of this world, unaided by God's Spirit, could never tell us. Paul makes this point strongly: "We speak the wisdom of God in a mystery, even the hidden wisdom, which God ordained before the world unto our glory: which none of the princes of this world knew" (1 Cor. 2:7–8). Indeed, the entire Bible reveals God's mysteries.

What Paul writes here shows how important it is that we be thoroughly informed about these mysteries. They are matters of the utmost importance and relevance to all persons and to all nations. These mysteries comprise aspects and elements of God's secret purposes of salvation which God "ordained before the world." These purposes of grace were drawn up by God for our highest good. As Paul puts it, they are "unto our glory."

The mysteries of God, therefore, are entirely different from the so-called "mysteries" of pagan religion or philosophy, which are nothing better than human guesswork painted over with a veneer of impressive superstition. God's mysteries, on the other hand, are His own eternal purposes by which He has given Christ as a Savior to mankind, and also the articles of faith which, if we believe, will give us eternal life with God in the glory of heaven.

The Mystery of God

The mystery of God.
—COLOSSIANS 2:2

God is the ultimate and most sublime mystery in all existence.[1] No being has ever equaled Him in majesty and sovereignty, and no being ever will. God's greatness is not relative or proportional but infinitely and transcendentally great. What we know of God in this life from a study of the Bible is accurate and true but is vastly less than what remains to be known of Him when we are with Him in heaven. In this life "we see through a glass darkly" (1 Cor. 13:12). The knowledge of God that awaits His people in the life to come is vastly greater than what the most learned scholars have attained to here below. In heaven God's children will see Him "face to face" and will enjoy Him to the uttermost forever.

All our knowledge of God in this life must be

---

1. The author gratefully acknowledges the guidance and help of his friend the Reverend Sherman Isbell in the writing of this chapter.

drawn principally from the Bible. There is a knowledge of God that is available from the created
universe. This knowledge is sufficient to render all
persons guilty who seek to suppress it in their minds.

However, the knowledge of God to be obtained
from a study of the natural world is not sufficient
to bring us as sinners to know and love Him as we
ought to do. Therefore, our knowledge of God must
be learned principally from what God tells us in
the Bible. It is what we learn from Scripture, either
explicitly or by good and necessary inference, that
must be allowed to shape and control our formu-
lation of the doctrine of God. What is drawn from
other sources will tend to mislead and so cloud our
understanding with a measure of idolatry.

The Holy Trinity

In the text quoted above from Paul's epistle to the
Colossians we gather that God's being, as the sacred
Trinity, is rightly looked on as a mystery. Paul's words
are, "The mystery of God, and of the Father, and of
Christ" (Col. 2:2). From other passages of Scripture
we learn that this mystery of the Trinity concerns the
Holy Spirit also. So these three holy persons of God
are to be looked on with wonder and worship. There
is profound mystery in this revealed truth: God is
one, yet in three persons. Let us attempt, following
the teaching of Scripture, to state the doctrine of God
more fully.

Defining the Doctrine of God

The three persons of the Holy Trinity—the Father, the Son, and the Holy Spirit—equally share one essence, or substance. Each of these three persons is God, but there are not three Gods. There is only one God. The names of the Father, Son, and Holy Spirit belong to the persons necessarily and are not the result of God's plan of redemption. In saying this we mean that whereas the existence and history of the universe are the result of God's purpose, will, and decree, God Himself is self-existent. He did not by a decree give being or form to Himself or to His own blessed persons.

God may be thought of in two ways. We may think of God as He is in Himself, and we may think of Him as He is related to the world which He has created. It is customary to refer to God in the first sense as the ontological Trinity, and in the second as the economic Trinity.

Within the ontological Trinity there are the following properties special to each person: the Father eternally begets the Son; the Son is eternally begotten of the Father; the Spirit eternally proceeds from the Father and from the Son. These properties belong to the eternal and necessary existence of God. They have no beginning, and they will have no end.

The Son of God and the Spirit are, like the Father, of themselves (the technical term which we use to express this truth is *autotheos*). The Son and the Spirit do not owe their origin or their being to

God the Father. Like the Father, they are eternal and uncreated.

The second person of the Holy Trinity is called the Son of God. In respect to His personal property of sonship, He is of the Father and in Scripture has the designation of the "only begotten Son" (John 3:16). In respect to His deity, He is of Himself God.

The Holy Spirit is the third person of the Trinity. In that He is the Holy Spirit, He proceeds from the Father and the Son. In that He is God, He is of Himself God.

While our definitions of God must always conform to the evidence of Scripture, our terminology may legitimately include words that are not found in Scripture. These words, such as the term *Trinity*, are used as necessary technical terms to convey accurate scriptural teaching about the being of God. Such technical terms are not wrong in that they express concepts that are entirely biblical.

The persons of the Godhead eternally indwell one another. The Father indwells the Son and the Spirit. The Son indwells the Father and the Spirit. The Spirit indwells the Father and the Son. The technical term we use to designate this mutual indwelling of the persons of the Godhead is the term *circumincession*.

The three persons of the Holy Trinity love one another and delight in one another. Each person perfectly and fully knows the other two persons. In Scripture, when one person refers to another it is with the utmost honor, respect, and affection. For example, the Father refers to Christ with these words: "This is my beloved Son, in whom I am well pleased" (Matt. 3:17). Christ says, "My Father is greater than I" (John 14:28). Jesus says the Holy Spirit "shall not speak of himself.... He shall glorify me" (John 16:13–14). The Spirit does not speak of Himself but of Christ.

The Economic Trinity

For the purposes of redemption these three blessed persons each have a work of their own. This refers to the economic Trinity. The Father's work is to send the Son, to call the elect, and to adopt them as His own dear children. The Son's work is to become incarnate of the Virgin Mary, to fulfill the moral law, to die for us on the cross, to rise from the dead, to ascend to heaven in order to intercede for us, and, at last, to come again to take believers home to glory. The Spirit's work is to give to Christ all needed strength for His ministry on earth, to regenerate the elect, to sanctify them in this world and so prepare them for heaven where they will be with God in glory eternally.

The soul of each believer enters into glory at the moment of death. There is no delay between a believer's death and his or her entrance into glory. We refer to this as the intermediate state.

The body and soul of each believer will enter into heaven together after the resurrection and the judgment. At the judgment each believer will receive praise and commendation from Christ, who will welcome us into glory. Believers will then take their places in the eternal world of heaven. We refer to this as the eternal state of the believer. Christ's love for believers is a special love arising from the fact that they are His bride, whom He has loved with an everlasting love and for whom He has paid the extremely great price of His own blood and sufferings while on the cross.

Our Duty of Love and Service to God

Believers make up Christ's church and are referred to in Scripture as His bride, bone of His bone and flesh of His flesh. Those who have Christ as their Savior also have God as their Father and the Spirit as their Comforter. Believers usually pray to the Father, through the Son as Mediator, and in the Spirit. However, prayer may be made to all three persons of the Godhead.

Our first and supreme duty is to love the Father, Son, and Holy Spirit with all our heart, soul, mind, and strength. God is to be worshiped only in the ways which He has commanded in His Word; to worship God in any way not commanded by Him in the Bible is vain and idolatrous. We are to receive the Bible as the inspired Word of God and as the only rule of faith and life.

It is our happy and blessed duty to meditate on this Holy Trinity with affection and gratitude, especially when we reflect on the gospel of saving grace. We are to trust in God and to rely on Him to supply all our needs, both temporal and eternal. We have the great honor of serving this holy God for the short time that we are on earth.

The ultimate joy we have as believers will be to see and to be with this blessed God—Father, Son, and Holy Spirit—in heaven forever. We refer to this glorious sight of God as the beatific vision. The beauty of God is infinite and surpasses all created beauty. The sight of God will ravish the hearts of believers forever in glory. The blessed vision of the triune God, together with a full enjoyment of His love to us in Christ, will be the chief source of our endless happiness as believers in the world to come.

Lessons to Learn from This Mystery of God

We should make it our great aim in this life to walk in fellowship with these three holy persons and to pray without ceasing to God. For God is able to carry us safely through this short life and to sanctify our experiences here on earth so that they might be profitable to us and to others, especially in matters of salvation.

We are to obey the will of the Holy Trinity as it is revealed in Scripture, especially in that we believe in the Lord Jesus Christ as our Savior and keep carefully God's moral law in public and in private. It is also our duty to seek to make known the truth of God to as many persons as possible so that they also may share with us the blessings of the gospel of Christ. Then we should seek to foster fellowship with those who share our precious faith, even though in this life we do not yet see eye to eye in all things. As Christians, we must promote love and joy among one another in this sad and fallen world.

Let us remember that the persons of the Holy Trinity cannot fail to bring to pass all that they have promised in Scripture and that as Christ, our great Head, is alive from the dead forevermore, so we who are believers will soon be with Him in glory. In this way, we can soften our own minds and those of our Christian brothers and sisters to that natural fear of death which tends to terrify us. This is possible when we remind ourselves that to be with Christ is far better than life in this present world. Let us then ever remember that as Christians we were once in a state of sin but are now redeemed by Christ; that we are now in a state of grace and are soon to be taken out of it at our death; and that after death we will pass from a state of grace to a state of glory, the most blessed state of all.

3

The Mystery of God's Covenant

The secret of the LORD is with them that fear him; and he will show them his covenant.

—PSALM 25:14

God has secrets He is pleased to reveal to some, but which most people never know. These secrets are among the mysteries we can only understand when we possess that fear of the Lord referred to in the text above. Among these secrets is the knowledge of God's covenant. It is a mystery, or secret, that is in our best interests to know because to be shown God's covenant is to enjoy His love in this life and in the life to come.

What is a covenant in the biblical sense? It is an arrangement that God makes with man which allows many to enjoy the favor and blessing of God in this life and the next. God will have no favorable relationship with any man unless he is in a right covenant standing before God.

When God makes a covenant with man He sets the terms and conditions, and He requires man to keep those conditions. If we adhere to God's required terms within His covenant He will bless us richly. If we break His covenant we must forfeit the blessing and expect to face the penalties, both in this life and in the life to come.

The Bible describes two covenants that are important for us to learn about and to ask God to help us understand. They are the covenant of works and the covenant of grace. God made the covenant of works at the beginning of history with our first father, Adam. Sometimes we call this the covenant of life. The terms and conditions of this covenant were that if Adam and Eve would obey God by refusing to eat the fruit of the Tree of Knowledge of Good and Evil, which was growing, like all other trees, in the garden of Eden, then God would bless them and give them eternal life. On the other hand, if our first parents should disobey God and eat of this tree, they would die. God's warning was very emphatic: "In the day that thou eatest thereof thou shalt surely die" (Gen. 2:17).

Adam and Eve knew clearly the terms of this covenant of works. But they broke the covenant and sinned against God. We refer to this extremely serious event as the fall. It brought all mankind into a condition of sin and misery. Had Adam not sinned, no one would ever die. We die because Adam broke the covenant. All the miseries of life, such as sickness, war, and poverty, have come upon this world as a just judgment from God for man's disobedience.

But why are we all punished for something that Adam did some six thousand years ago? Here we see how mystery attaches to the covenants God has made with mankind. The explanation is that Adam was the representative of us all within this covenant of works. He was what we call technically a "covenant head." That is to say, he acted on behalf of all mankind when he disobeyed and broke the covenant God made with man. The effects upon every one of us are extremely serious. Because Adam broke the covenant, all men are born in a sinful state in these three ways: first, the guilt of Adam's sin is imputed to us all from the moment of our conception; second, we are all born without the righteousness that Adam had at his creation; and third, we are born with a nature that is corrupt and inclined to evil.

The breaking of the covenant of works explains why the world is the place it is, full of crime, cruelty, and exploitation. If Adam had kept the covenant's conditions, nothing miserable or unpleasant would have entered into man's life. Moreover, if Adam had never sinned against God, there would be no death. Man would have lived forever in a state of happiness, enjoying unbroken fellowship with God and all the comforts of an unspoiled world. But, because Adam did not keep the covenant of works, that did not happen.

Mercifully, it was not the will of God that the world should perish. He has revealed to mankind another covenant, which we refer to as the covenant of grace. The word grace means God's unmerited favor. What

God teaches us in revealing to us the nature of the covenant of grace is wonderful in every way.

As we read what the Bible has to tell us about the covenant of grace, we discover this: from all eternity God had appointed Jesus Christ to be a second Adam who would stand as the representative of His people. Christ, as "the last Adam" (1 Cor. 15:45), would represent those whom God had given to Him before the world began. He would do this in order to save them from the state of sin and death.

To save His people, Christ had to become man and die for us. By living and dying as our covenant Head, the Lord Jesus would pay the price required to satisfy God's injured justice for the sins of His people. Our Savior lived His entire life to fulfill God's moral law for us as our covenant representative. He kept every commandment perfectly. His entire life was sinless and obedient.

All the sins of God's people were imputed to Christ when He was on the cross. His death was intimately related to the covenant of grace. This is why, on the night before He died, He referred to the wine of the Lord's Supper in this way: "This is my blood of the new testament, which is shed for many for the remission of sins" (Matt. 26:28). The words *testament* and *covenant* both refer to the same thing: God's covenant of grace.

The New Testament contrasts Christ with Adam. Both are heads of a covenant that God has made with men. Whereas Adam failed, Christ triumphed.

Whereas Adam lost for us the fellowship and favor of God, Christ restores it for all who trust in Him as their Savior. Whereas Adam's disobedience brought sin, condemnation, and death to the entire world, Christ brought righteousness, justification, and eternal life. The apostle Paul develops this contrast between Adam and Christ in Romans 5:12–19. Here he wonderfully draws aside the curtain that once concealed this great mystery of the covenants.

Indeed, the love of God in the provisions of the new covenant does not stop there. Adam, by his one sin, was the occasion of our death, and now Christ, by His death and resurrection, is the occasion of our eternal life. He is our forerunner, the Savior who has risen from the grave and is now seated in glory. "For as in Adam all die, even so in Christ shall all be made alive. But every man in his own order: Christ the firstfruits; afterwards they that are Christ's at his coming. Then cometh the end, when he shall have delivered up the kingdom to God, even the Father" (1 Cor. 15:22–24).

Adam brought a moral disturbance into the world, a disturbance that challenged the absolute sovereignty and lordship of God. But when Christ, at the end, defeats every foe, He will vindicate God's insulted majesty. In the new heaven and new earth, God will be "all in all" (1 Cor. 15:28), and all His creatures will see Him as such. So Christ, in the end, will reverse the catalog of evils that Adam intro-duced into the world when he committed his first sin as the representative of mankind within the covenant of works.

The terms and conditions of the covenant of grace are what we call the gospel. The gospel requires these two conditions of us: that we repent of our sins, and that we believe in the Lord Jesus Christ as the only Savior of the world, outside of whom there is no salvation for anyone. It is clear, then, that God calls us to trust in Jesus Christ for salvation and peace with Himself.

Throughout human history, Christ has been the Savior. Adam and Eve heard of Christ after they had sinned, for God revealed to them that He would come as the "seed" of the woman to bruise the head of the serpent (Gen. 3:15). Paul's words make it clear that this is a prophecy of Christ: "The God of peace shall bruise Satan under your feet shortly" (Rom. 16:20). Those who believe in Christ will be saved. But those who do not believe in Him as their own personal Savior will be lost. This is the serious implication for the nonbeliever. He is still in a relationship with God that flows from the consequences of Adam's sin. The unbeliever is in a broken covenant relationship with his Maker. The guilt of Adam's sin has been imputed to him. If he does not repent and come by faith to Christ, he will enter into eternal punishment at his death.

To die as one of Christ's people is to die within the terms of the covenant of grace. To die as an unbeliever is to die within the terms of the broken covenant of works, which carries the sentence of eternal death. Our Lord Jesus Christ frequently preached that there will be eternal punishment for everyone who rejects His gospel.

God is very gracious. He has no pleasure in the death of sinners, and He therefore invites all who hear the gospel to come to Jesus Christ for eternal life. The "secret" God teaches those who fear Him is just this: "He that believeth on [Jesus] is not condemned; but he that believeth not is condemned already" (John 3:18). Those whom God teaches by His grace come to understand that Christ is the Savior of the world. They come to Him and find eternal life. This is what it means: "The secret of the LORD is with them that fear him; and he will show them his covenant" (Ps. 25:14). Have you understood this mystery?

4

The Mystery of Godliness

Great is the mystery of godliness: God was manifest in the flesh.

—1 TIMOTHY 3:16

Of all God's wonderful works, it is surely impossible to find any greater than the birth of Jesus Christ. Every birth of a human child is wonderful, but Christ's birth is uniquely great and glorious. It is unique in several ways. First, Jesus was born without sin. He is the only child who has ever been born sinless. Also, He is the only man who existed before He was conceived and born into the world. This truth reminds us that Jesus was not only a human child; He was the eternal Son of God. Also, He did not come into the world to enjoy life but to live, suffer, and die for others. He came into our human nature to save us from our sins. This is the meaning of His name, Jesus. The Bible tells us: "Thou shalt call his name JESUS: for he shall save his people from their sins" (Matt. 1:21).

The technical term for the birth of Christ is the word *incarnation,* which means "coming into flesh."

This word expresses the fact that Jesus Christ existed before His birth as God the Son, the second person of the glorious Godhead. As the Son of God, Christ had no beginning. He was not created or made, but, like God the Father, He has existed eternally and always will. However, at the incarnation, Jesus Christ, who previously existed as God, also became man. Therefore, we refer to Christ as the God-man. This says something most amazing. Since the incarnation occurred, Jesus Christ has existed as one person in two natures. He is both God and man. These two natures are not mixed with each other. They are distinct from each other, but they are also in union with one another. Jesus is fully God and also truly man.

All God's works are wonderful and should stir up adoration and love for God in our hearts. Such works include God's creation, providence, judgment, and future re-creation of the present universe. But surely none of God's works is more amazing than the incarnation, in which God Himself became united with our human nature in the person of the Lord Jesus Christ. In taking our human nature in this way, God has honored us above angels—indeed, above all other orders of creation. How grateful we should be that Almighty God should visit us—and even put on our nature by becoming man!

Let us be clear about what exactly the incarnation means. First we must understand that God became man not by subtraction but by addition. In other words, Christ did not cast off His Godhood and replace it with humanity. Rather, He retained His Godhood and united our human nature to it. So Christ did not cease to be God when He became man. A famous early Christian writer, Athanasius, expressed it well: "He became what He was not, without ceasing to be what He was."

Of course, the incarnation was a miracle. Jesus, as the Bible makes clear in both the Old and the New Testaments, was born supernaturally. He had a mother but no human father. His mother, Mary, conceived the human nature of Jesus not from Joseph but from the creative power of the Holy Spirit of God. So the Bible says, "A virgin shall conceive, and bear a son" (Isa. 7:14; Matt. 1:23). As to His manhood, Christ had no father, and as to His Godhood, He had no mother.

Some refer to Mary as the "mother of God," but this expression can be misleading. She was the mother of the human nature of the Son of God but not the mother of His Godhood. We honor Mary as the chosen vessel of God to birth the perfect and sinless human nature of Jesus. Elizabeth refers to Mary as "the mother of my Lord" (Luke 1:43), but this meaning is to be limited to the human nature of Jesus.

We must honor Mary for the fact that she was, out of all the women who have ever lived, selected by God to be the mother of Christ's human nature. But we must not superstitiously venerate Mary as if she were more than human. She was a virgin when Jesus was born, but she must have had normal relations with her husband, Joseph, after the birth of Jesus. The Bible makes this quite clear: "Joseph...knew her not till she had brought forth her firstborn son: and he called his name JESUS" (Matt. 1:25).

The birth of Christ began a chain of wonderful events that mark it as extremely important for mankind. One of these events was the coming of certain "wise men from the east" (Matt. 2:1). God caused them to follow a star to Jerusalem to the exact place where our Lord was at that time with His mother (Matt. 2:11). On finding the baby Jesus they "fell down, and worshipped him" (Matt. 2:11) and presented valuable gifts to Him. No doubt this event was a sign that Christ had come to open the door of salvation to all nations, Gentiles as well as Jews. It was an event of great significance. When Christ had, thirty-three years later, completed His work, the Spirit of God came down at Pentecost, and Gentiles all over the world began to flood into the kingdom of God.

Another significant event had occurred earlier: the coming of the shepherds to the manger where Christ lay (Luke 2:16). This event took place on the very night of Christ's birth, when the angel of the Lord was sent to announce Christ's birth to the shepherds. We note that the angel was sent to humble shepherds and not to proud Pharisees. God honors those who are of a humble heart and have faith in His Word, not those who are proud.

This event indicated the glorious and earth-shaking importance of Christ's birth. The child who was born in the manger was none other than the long-promised Messiah: "Unto you is born this day in the city of David a Saviour, which is Christ the Lord" (Luke 2:11). Indeed, the incarnation was so important to the whole of mankind that a multitude of angels appeared that night with a song of praise that must have made the heavens ring: "Glory to God in the highest, and on earth peace, good will toward men" (Luke 2:14).

Why did the Son of God take our human nature? It was in order to save us poor sinners. As He put it Himself, "I came not to call the righteous, but sinners to repentance" (Mark 2:17; Luke 5:32).

Jesus was sinless. He was not under Adam's broken covenant of works, as we all are. Hence the sin of Adam was never imputed to Him. To save us, He had to be without sin, and He had to live and also die for us. Therefore He had to have a human nature in which He might both live an obedient life and die an atoning death for us.

A mere man could not live and die for us since his life and death could never merit salvation. Therefore, in the marvelous wisdom of God, Christ needed to be both God and man. As a man, He was able to live under the moral law and so achieve a perfect life. As a man, He was able, in His love, to die for us and to merit forgiveness by satisfying the justice of God and so make peace for all who would believe in Him. Hence Christ must be both man and God. As a man,

He lived and died for us. As God, He gave infinite value to His life and His death.

By life and death Christ obtained a perfect righteousness for all those who believe in Him. There are two aspects of Christ's obedience. We refer to them as His active obedience and His passive obedience. By these terms we refer to the perfection of His earthly life and the merit of His atoning death.

Christ, in His life and death, was acting as the representative of all His believing people. As our representative, He obtained a righteousness that He can bestow on all Christian believers. By His life He fully satisfied all the requirements of the Ten Commandments for us. And by His agonies and death He satisfied all the claims of God's offended justice. Thus He is "the Lord our Righteousness," as the Old Testament prophesied that He would be (Jer. 23:6).

Christ has, and ever will have, two natures. Yet He is one person, whom we should trust and love with deepest gratitude in view of His love for us needy sinners. As the God-man, He now sits "in the midst of the throne" of Almighty God. His work is to govern all nations and to call out by the gospel all whom God eternally gave to Him. "Great is the mystery of godliness"!

5

The Mystery of the Gospel

We speak the wisdom of God in a mystery.
—1 CORINTHIANS 2:7

To make known the mystery of the gospel.
—EPHESIANS 6:19

The apostle Paul describes the gospel of our Lord and Savior Jesus Christ as a mystery. This in no way means that the gospel is obscure or difficult to understand. Paul's meaning is that the gospel is a divinely revealed method of salvation that the mind of man could never know without God revealing it to us.

To clarify his meaning, the apostle uses an illustration: "What man knoweth the things of a man, save the spirit of man which is in him?" (1 Cor. 2:11). Paul's meaning is obvious. We cannot read the secret thoughts of others until they are revealed to us. In the same way, we could never know God's secret thoughts if He had not revealed them to us. This He has graciously done in the Bible.

The gospel, then, is not a message that comes to us from the intellects of great men. Indeed, the greatest intellects of history never imagined that the way of salvation would be what God has shown it to be in His Word. The gospel was "ordained before the world unto our glory" (1 Cor. 2:7). The total and complete ignorance of this gospel on the part of the eminent intellectuals of the past is made manifest in that they crucified Christ, "the Lord of glory" (1 Cor. 2:8). Had the great men of the past known who Christ was and what He came to do by His blessed death on the cross, they would never have put Him to death as they did. The point is proved. The gospel is God's secret plan of salvation. It is a mystery that the unaided minds of men, even clever men, could never have invented.

That the gospel of Christ is a mystery is also clear from the fact that people regard it as "foolishness" (1 Cor. 2:14) until God opens their eyes to give them spiritual understanding. Until God enlightens our minds by His gracious Holy Spirit we all remain in the darkness of unbelief so far as Christ's gospel is concerned. This fact explains why it is, and ever has been, that so many reject the Christian faith and in some cases openly scoff at it. The mystery of the gospel is a subject of contempt until God shines His light into our hearts to make it precious to us.

Clearly, God's method of salvation is very different from what mankind expects it to be. At the heart of all forms of false religion is the belief that salvation is obtained by works. In every nation on the earth, the instinct of self-righteousness is so strong in fallen man that he always tries to be acceptable to God through his own deeds. These deeds may include prayers, rituals, sacraments, sacrifices, acts of charity, or self-inflicted punishments. All non-Christian religions look for acceptance with God (or some concept of God) in one of these ways. Sadly, many who claim to belong to the Christian church make the same mistake. It was the tragic error of the Jews in the time of Christ. Hence Paul says of the Jews of his day: "Israel, which followed after righteousness, hath not attained to the law of righteousness. Wherefore? Because they sought it not by faith, but as it were by the works of the law" (Rom. 9:31–32).

Indeed, Paul himself, who here refers to the gospel as a mystery, was entirely blind to the true way of salvation until he met Christ on the Damascus road (Acts 9). But when the scales fell from his eyes, he not only revised but totally reversed his doctrine of salvation. Once Christ opened Paul's mind to the truth of the New Testament gospel he viewed his former self-righteousness with the most vehement hatred: "What things were gain to me, those I counted loss for Christ.... [I] do count them but dung, that I may win Christ" (Phil. 3:7–8).

Everything about the gospel is a surprise to us when we are first converted. The truths of salvation dawn upon us as light from another world. At the center of it all is the sovereign love of God who has sent a Savior into this world to rescue us from our hopeless plight as guilty sinners. By faith we now see

Jesus, not as once we did—a great figure of history perhaps, or a religious genius only—but as our own beloved personal Savior who died for us on the cross.

As our understanding grows, we come to see more fully what Paul means when he says that Jesus Christ "is made unto us wisdom, and righteousness, and sanctification, and redemption" (1 Cor. 1:30). The glorious truth about the gospel is that Christ has done everything for us. We enter into peace with God by faith alone in Him whom God appointed to be our Redeemer, Christ the Lord.

When Paul tells us that Christ is our "wisdom, and righteousness, and sanctification, and redemption" (1 Cor. 1:30), he is giving us a digest of God's way of salvation. Each of these terms is rich in meaning, and each reveals to us one aspect or another of the gospel mystery of salvation.

How is Christ our "wisdom"? He becomes our wisdom when, as sinners, our eyes are opened to see ourselves as God sees us. The tragic truth is that none of us realizes our serious plight until God breaks into our darkness and stops us in our tracks. Our natural instinct is to live for the pleasures of this world and ignore the fact of death. But when God begins to give us the wisdom that we here speak about, He takes measures to arrest us in our mad rush for vain pleasure. Often God has to be cruel to be kind. We are so foolish and blind that we sprint headlong toward a lost eternity until God stops us. This He may do in various ways, including by illness, by bereavement, by a sermon, by the testimony of a Christian friend, or by a book about the gospel.

The wisdom God gives us when He takes measures to bring us to Christ is a new realization that we dare not live any longer without putting our trust in Christ as our personal Savior. Often it is with tears that the sinner is brought to this point of self-despair. He feels an influence upon him that he may not at first be able to explain. But sooner or later he comes to know that the constraint on his mind, will, and conscience was the call of God to him. He now turns his face to seek God's pardon, whatever the cost may be in terms of the loss of worldly friends or the esteem of worldly companions. Gospel wisdom makes all who have it put God's will first in their life. From then on everything else comes second.

How does Christ become our "righteousness"? The only correct way to understand this aspect of the gospel mystery is to appreciate what is meant by the technical term *imputation*. This word means that when the sinner puts his faith in Christ as his Savior for the very first time, the righteousness of Christ is imputed to him. God reckons the righteousness of Christ to be that of the believing sinner. By faith alone the sinner is now justified in the sight of God.

To the unbelieving critic of the gospel this is always an offensive doctrine. He cannot think it is right that God should require no more of us than to have faith in Jesus. This doctrine of the gospel is unquestionably a mystery to the nonbeliever. But it is the clear teaching of the Bible that faith in Christ alone brings pardon of all sins and a guarantee of eternal life in heaven to any man.

We must not imagine that good works on our part are required to supplement the righteousness of Christ. The fact is that Christ's life and death have purchased for sinners a perfect and eternal righteousness. The means by which a sinner receives this righteousness is faith and faith alone in Jesus Christ. So Paul makes it clear that "by grace are ye saved through faith; and that not of yourselves; it is the gift of God: not of works, lest any man should boast" (Eph. 2:8–9). The apostle Paul emphasizes this again and again in his epistles. Neither Paul nor Martin Luther nor any other unconverted person ever understood this gospel mystery until they came to know what it is to be right with God through their own experience. Justification is truly a great mystery of the gospel of Christ.

How is Christ our "sanctification"? This is the third element of Paul's great gospel summary in 1 Corinthians 1:30. Sanctification differs from justification. Whereas justification refers to the sinner's legal standing before God, sanctification refers to the change brought about in the life and character of the individual believer.

Sanctification alters our whole moral character. At our conversion we begin to be new men and women. Our whole attitude changes. Before conversion we lived to please ourselves. After conversion, when we believe in Christ, we wish to please God. Indeed, we see it to be our duty to live to the glory of God and not for personal pleasure.

So, where justification refers to our legal standing before God, sanctification refers to the inward change in us. The Christian is now no longer what he was. He was, before conversion, what the Bible calls the "old man" (Col. 3:9–10).

Justification takes place instantaneously the moment the sinner believes in Christ. He is now credited with the obedience of Jesus, so he is now not guilty. He is pardoned of all sin forever and is beyond the possibility of being condemned in the day of death or on the judgment day.

In contrast, sanctification is a lifelong process. The converted believer grows in grace. He is called upon by God to "work out [his] salvation with fear and trembling" (Phil. 2:12). Gradually, by the Spirit's grace, he learns to mortify evil thoughts and unholy practices. In this way he adds to his faith and grows in holiness. However, the believer will have indwelling sin in his life all his days. Sanctification is never complete in this life.

How is Christ our "redemption"? This term that Paul uses in explaining the gospel mystery refers to the state of moral perfection that every true believer will achieve at death. It is the moral and spiritual goal he aims at all his life. The greatest Christians are still imperfect in this life, but they strive after perfection as far as they can. Paul can refer to his own spiritual state in this way: "I count not myself to have apprehended.... I press toward the mark for the prize of the high calling of God in Christ Jesus" (Phil. 3:13–14).

At death the soul of the believer is made perfect. The soul enters into heaven. The body is placed in the grave. In the great day of resurrection the soul and body will be reunited. Then we will stand before Christ as our great Judge. Every believer will then be welcomed by Him to the eternal joys of heaven. What a glorious mystery the gospel is! All praise and glory be to God.

6

The Mystery of the New Birth

How can a man be born when he is old?

—JOHN 3:4

God describes the unbeliever as the "old man" (Col. 3:9). On the other hand, when he comes to faith in the Lord Jesus Christ he is said to be a "new man" (Col. 3:10). This teaching clearly shows that there is a world of difference between what a person is before conversion and what he is after conversion. To become a true Christian is not merely to believe a new set of doctrines, or to adjust one's habits to fit a different lifestyle. The real Christian is radically different from all unbelievers. More wonderful still, he is different from what he himself once was. Before conversion he is the "old man"; after coming to Jesus Christ by faith he becomes a "new man."

All life begins with birth. Where there is no birth, there is no life. This is true both physically and spiritually. The transition of a person from "old man" to "new man" is brought about by a spiritual rebirth. We refer to this as the *new birth*, or the *second birth*.

So for any sinner to become a saved sinner he must be born again, as our Lord explains to Nicodemus, a devout but unconverted Jewish Pharisee (John 3).

The new birth is a mystery to all of us until we have this experience of being reborn. It is good to have religious knowledge and a moral lifestyle restrained by biblical knowledge, but no man is a true Christian until he has entered into this wonderful spiritual change that the Bible calls the new birth. What is it? How can we seek it? What difference will it make in our life? Let us look at Christ's interview with Nicodemus, recorded in John 3.

It was a remarkable thing for Nicodemus, a prominent Pharisee, to have come to Jesus as he did. The Pharisees were a proud sect. Their idea of pleasing God was by a strict keeping of rules, some of which were biblical and some of which were man-made. They attempted to be right with God on the basis of their own self-righteousness, and they looked down on others. Christ exposed them for their hypocrisy and blindness (Matt. 23:23–24). Their holier-than-thou attitude had long before been prophesied by Isaiah, who depicted these self-righteous men speaking in this way: "Stand by thyself, come not near to me; for I am holier than thou" (Isa. 65:5). Such a proud attitude, of course, is very offensive to God.

Nicodemus came to Jesus by night (John 3:2). This detail is significant and is referred to on each occasion in which Nicodemus is mentioned (John 7:50; 19:39). Evidently he came by night to avoid being seen by others. To be seen making a visit to Christ was to risk losing the good opinion of his fellow religionists. It was a price he would rather not pay—at least not yet, not at that point in his life. So he sought a private, confidential interview with Jesus by night.

The question presses itself upon us: Why did he come at all if he risked losing friends? The answer is part of the mystery attached to the new birth. Nicodemus came because God was beginning to "draw him" (John 6:44). The miracles of Christ that he had heard about (John 3:2) were in his mind and conscience bearing testimony to Christ's divine person and heaven-appointed authority as the Messiah. Nicodemus did not yet know it, but he came to Christ to learn more about Him because God's secret will and purpose was for Nicodemus to become a Christian. He did not yet realize it himself, but the true explanation as to why he came to Jesus by night was that God was beginning to direct him to the place where he would find true religion and come to reject his Pharisaism.

Jesus, in this interview, immediately announces to Nicodemus what every man needs if he is to get true religion: "Except a man be born again, he cannot see the kingdom of God" (John 3:3). The word "see" here means that a person who has not experienced the new birth is blind to the true meaning of the Bible and therefore cannot begin to understand his own need as a sinner nor grasp the nature of

God's church. The real church, or "kingdom of God," is made up of born-again people and no others. It is for that reason that we use the term *invisible church*. Although unconverted persons may be members of the visible church, they cannot, without a second birth, belong to the *real* invisible church of God's saved people.

To Nicodemus and to every other unconverted person this sounds absurd. "How can a man be born when he is old?" asks Nicodemus, to which our Lord replies that to enter God's kingdom, every man must be "born of water and of the Spirit" (John 3:5). It is most important to grasp the true meaning of our Lord's words here. There is no reference to baptism intended by the term "water." The proof of this is that water cannot cleanse the soul of anyone. Rather, this reference to water was an allusion to a teaching in the Old Testament which, as a devout Jew, Nicodemus well knew, or ought to have known. The water Christ speaks of is the cleansing of the heart by the gracious work of God's Holy Spirit. This water is the only kind that can purify a man's soul and make him "whiter than snow" (Ps. 51:7). In reference to this water, the prophet Ezekiel, describing the new birth, stated, "Then will I sprinkle clean water upon you, and ye shall be clean: from all your filthiness, and from all your idols, will I cleanse you" (Ezek. 36:25).

The sinner is "dead in trespasses and sins" (Eph. 2:1). His great need is to be brought into a condition of spiritual life. So Christ goes on to say to

Nicodemus, "That which is born of the flesh is flesh" (John 3:6). However, sinners can be delivered from this fearful condition of spiritual death by a gracious work of God's Holy Spirit. "That which is born of the Spirit is spirit" (John 3:6). The agent in this spiritual change is the third person of the blessed Trinity, who is, like the wind, full of power.

Christ compares the Spirit's work in the new birth to the activity of the wind (v. 8): "The wind bloweth where it listeth," that is, where it wishes. There is no exterior power that can control the wind. It is powerful and outside of man's ability to direct or manage. So it is with the Holy Spirit. Like the wind, He is powerful and invisible. He works in men's hearts as He is pleased to do. None can compel or restrain Him.

How then can we know when the Holy Spirit is at work in a person's life? By the changes that can be seen in a man's soul. We see the wind not directly but indirectly, by the movement it causes in the trees. Even so, the Holy Spirit brings about visible changes in the soul of a man or woman. A born-again man is a new man. He is a new edition of his former self.

These changes are not merely outward, like an old cottage that has been newly whitewashed. The changes are basic, fundamental, and radical. Every faculty of the soul is affected. The dishonest man becomes honest. The thief steals no more. The man who formerly used bad language now has a clean tongue. The lazy idler now applies himself to his work. The careless mother now starts to train up

her children in the ways of the Lord. The thought-
less pleasure-seeker now begins to read his Bible and
attend the house of God. The new man really *is* new.
It is a new birth.

We say that a converted person is a new man. In
what does this newness consist? The supernatural
power of God so changes a new believer that he or
she is now in fellowship with God and has become
His child. When we are born, we are sinful and at
enmity with God. When we are reborn, we become
children of God. God is now our spiritual Father as
well as our Creator.

The new birth alters our entire attitude toward
God and the things that belong to God. Whereas
before the new birth we have little interest in God
or in the things of God, after our rebirth, God, and
all that relates to God, becomes the supreme interest and concern of our whole life. This is so because
the instinct of every born-again person is to love God
and to wish to please Him.

Nicodemus shows by his subsequent behavior
that he is a changed man. He now speaks up for
Christ and in defense of Him (John 7:50–51). He is
now not ashamed to show deep respect for the body
of the crucified Redeemer: "There came also Nicodemus, which at the first came to Jesus by night,
and brought a mixture of myrrh and aloes, about
a hundred pound weight" (John 19:39). This was
an expensive gift. To this act of love Nicodemus,
together with Joseph of Arimathea, adds still more:

"Then took they the body of Jesus, and wound it in linen clothes with the spices, as the manner of the Jews is to bury" (John 19:40).

Nicodemus's love and respect for Christ flow from his experience of the new birth, to which, until recently, he had been a stranger. It is so with all who believe in Christ. They have faith in Him and love for Him. They have been drawn by the Father to know that Jesus is the only Savior of the world. They have heard the call of God in their soul. Now they are in living relationship with God and are being taught to "put off the old man" and to "put on the new man" (Col. 3:9–10).

Those who are born again are truly holy and they love holiness. Their wish is to be perfect. But so long as they are in this present life they have to contend with indwelling sin in themselves. Their cry is: "O wretched man that I am! who shall deliver me from the body of this death?" (Rom. 7:24). But in the instant of physical death their soul enters into glory.

7

The Mystery of Christ's Glorious Indwelling

The riches of the glory of this mystery…which is Christ in you.

—COLOSSIANS 1:27

Everyone who truly believes in Jesus Christ is in union with Christ. Not only is it true that Christ lived and died for us, and not only is it true that Christ now intercedes for us, but Christ also dwells in our soul. A number of Scripture passages teach of this wonderful indwelling. In the passage above, Paul uses very strong and exalted language. He speaks of this indwelling of Christ as a mystery that is richly glorious: "The riches of the glory of this mystery." Such high speech must be an indication that the doctrine now before us is full of importance and is therefore most necessary for us to seek to understand. The indwelling of Christ in the souls of His people is a great privilege for us. We are, after all, ruined and fallen sinners deserving to be cast away from God's presence.

But, far from casting us off, God has been pleased to make a home in our hearts! That He has done this is a kindness to us in every way. If Christ is in us, then sin will not have dominion over us (Rom. 6:14). If Christ is in us, then we have a sure and immoveable hope of being with Him in heaven at last, for He is "the hope of glory" (Col. 1:27). If Christ is in us, then we must be victorious over all our enemies (Rom. 8:37–39). If Christ be in us, then we shall have a taste of His love all our days until we see His blessed face in heaven (1 Cor. 13:12).

The Bible uses various illustrations to convey to us the nature and importance of Christ's indwelling in the souls of His people. Jesus Himself uses the illustration of a vine and its branches (John 15). As the sap nourishes the branch and enables it to bring forth fruit, so does Christ in the believer by His Spirit. As the expert vine-dresser skillfully prunes each branch so that it may be more fruitful, so does our heavenly Father. As every unfruitful and dead branch is cut away from the vine and cast into the fire, so does God remove—sooner or later—each merely nominal believer. The proof, therefore, of being a true Christian is not merely in our character and life. Love and service to God and man are the real evidence of our being true Christians.

The apostles Paul and Peter use the illustration of a building to convey aspects of our union with Christ. As believers, we "are built upon the foundation of the apostles and prophets, Jesus Christ himself being the chief corner stone;…in whom ye also are builded together for a habitation of God through the Spirit"

(Eph. 2:20, 22). Converted men and women, says Peter, are "as lively [living] stones...built up a spiritual house, a holy priesthood, to offer up spiritual sacrifices, acceptable to God by Jesus Christ" (1 Peter 2:5). The teaching here is to the effect that the church is indwelt by God, and every separate stone is a vital entity in the church, which is constantly growing and will be complete when all God's chosen people come at last to the knowledge of Christ as the foundation of their lives.

A third illustration is that of the head and the body. Paul uses this illustration: "[God] hath put all things under his feet, and gave him to be the head over all things to the church, which is his body, the fulness of him that filleth all in all" (Eph. 1:22–23). Again, the apostle Paul writes, "As the body is one, and hath many members, and all the members of that one body, being many, are one body: so also is Christ" (1 Cor. 12:12). Christ is the Head of the church and the one who controls every member of it. As Christians we are to be submissive to Christ's headship and to respect and honor our fellow believers as members of His mystical body, the church.

Perhaps the most amazing illustration of Christ's union with His people is that of a husband and wife within the marriage relationship: "For this cause shall a man leave his father and mother and shall be joined unto his wife, and they two shall be one flesh. This is a great mystery: but I speak concerning Christ and the church" (Eph. 5:31–32). Similarly, the apostle John describes the spiritual relationship of the church with her Lord and Savior: "I John saw the holy city, new Jerusalem, coming down from God out of heaven, prepared as a bride adorned for her husband" (Rev. 21:2). As believers we are united with Christ now, and we are to enjoy a blessed eternity with our God-man Redeemer.

In light of the teaching implied in these illustrations, it is no wonder that Paul refers to the believer's union with Christ as a mystery that possesses the "riches of the glory" (Col. 1:27)! We refer to this union of believers to Christ as the mystical union. Mystical union is comprised of both union and communion. *Union* is the term for the relationship as such; *communion* refers to our conscious enjoyment of Christ's presence and His love. Our union is forever, and it is unbreakable. It does not fluctuate or vary. But the experience of our enjoyment of our relationship with Christ does vary. There are times when we feel Christ near, and there are other times when we, perhaps because of sin, lose a felt sense of His fellowship.

In heaven we will have unbroken fellowship with Christ, but so long as we are in this life, because of our indwelling sin, we experience times of spiritual withdrawal of Christ's love. David, when he had sinned, felt the loss of Christ's presence and cried out, "Restore unto me the joy of thy salvation" (Ps. 51:12).

The indwelling of Christ's Holy Spirit is the source of our joy. Hence, in his sad and guilty state, David exclaimed, "Take not thy Holy Spirit from me" (Ps. 51:11). The union we have with our Lord and Savior is unchangeable; but our enjoyment of that union rises and falls. We refer to this variable factor as our communion with Christ. The Song of Solomon explains how our sense of Christ's nearness and love may be dimmed for a time—and shows us that our duty is to seek after Christ by secret prayer: "By night on my bed I sought him whom my soul loveth: I sought him, but I found him not. I will rise now, and…seek him whom my soul loveth" (Song 3:1–2).

As believers we need to see that we were given to Christ by the Father in eternity past. Our Lord refers to this in His great High Priestly Prayer: "I have manifested thy name unto the men which thou gavest me out of the world: thine they were, and thou gavest them me" (John 17:6). This is the origin of our special relationship with Christ as believers. But we do not enter into the experience of it until we are born again. At our new birth we come to know and love Christ. This union we now have with Him continues throughout life and will be enjoyed fully and perfectly at last when Christ returns and we enter with Him into the new heavens and the new earth.

Our Lord prays for us with this future eternal glory in mind when He says to the Father: "Father, I will that they also, whom thou hast given me, be with me where I am; that they may behold my glory…that the love wherewith thou hast loved me may be in them, and I in them" (John 17:24, 26). So the mystical union we have with Christ is a foretaste of heaven itself. "Behold, the tabernacle of God is with men, and he will dwell with them, and they shall be his people, and God himself shall be with them, and be their God" (Rev. 21:3).

If we have Christ dwelling in us as our hope of glory (Col. 1:27) we will have experiences that others do not have. For one thing, the world will hate us (John 15:18–19). This is to be expected because those who are not Christ's are the enemies of God, and, though they may not believe it, Satan works in them because, as unbelievers, they are "children of disobedience." We must expect the world to hate those whose hearts are indwelt by the triune God since the world rejects the gospel and all who speak up for God.

Our present task in this world is to order and organize our lives to live for God's glory. The indwelling of Christ's Spirit in our hearts is the source of all spiritual growth, progress, and acceptable service. Since this is so, we must strive to grow in the knowledge of God and to add to our faith every virtue and every grace, especially the grace of Christian love.

Love is the greatest of all graces (1 Cor. 13:13), and it greatly glorifies God when His people show forth the love of kindness in their lives. After all, what does it mean to be indwelt by Christ but that we should be increasingly conformed to His likeness?

This lifestyle and character of kindness and love is the badge of true Christianity. People may scoff at what we believe, but in their conscience they will recognize that we have what they do not have. They will see that we live and walk in fellowship with Jesus.

8

The Mystery of the Gospel Offer

Whosoever will, let him take the water of life freely.
—REVELATION 22:17

I thank thee, O Father, Lord of heaven and earth, because thou hast hid these things from the wise and prudent.
—MATTHEW 11:25

The gospel is the good news that Jesus Christ came into the world to save sinners. This gospel is to be preached to "every creature" (Mark 16:15) according to the command of Christ Himself. All who hear the gospel are invited to believe and come to Christ. Those who hear the summons of this gospel are to be assured that, if they wish to come to Christ, they will be welcomed by Him. "Him that cometh to me," says Jesus, "I will in no wise cast out" (John 6:37).

In these New Testament times, all nations are bidden to come to the living God and to be blessed with the eternal life which Christ died to procure for us. There never has been and never will be a situation in which any sinner who truly longs to be saved is repulsed by God. "Whosoever shall call upon the name of the Lord shall be saved" (Rom. 10:13).

It is, therefore, the duty of the preacher to urge every person who hears him to repent and to believe in Christ. John the Baptist's message to Israel at the close of the Old Testament era was that men should repent in order to receive "the remission of sins" (Mark 1:4). Similarly, Christ, when He began to preach, proclaimed this message: "The time is fulfilled, and the kingdom of God is at hand: repent ye, and believe the gospel" (Mark 1:15). Some time later the apostle Paul, preaching at Athens, announced: "God...now commandeth all men every where to repent" (Acts 17:30).

Therefore, the message we call the gospel is a summons issued by God, through the mouth of the preacher, whereby He commands all men to repent, turn from their sinful ways, and believe in Jesus Christ. Along with this authoritative command come God's assurance and His certain promise that all who do believe will be welcomed, accepted, and pardoned eternally.

This offer of pardon by God is genuine and sincere. No sinner is so wicked that God will reject him if he comes with a penitent heart, because the offer of a free pardon is sincerely made by God to all who hear it. It should be evident to every reader of the Bible that God cannot be insincere in any promise or offer He makes. Men may make insincere offers, but the God of heaven cannot possibly do such a thing. The vilest sinner on earth may have a free pardon if only he will believe God's promise in the gospel and humbly submit his life to Christ.

At this point we must admit that we meet with mystery. This mystery lies in two considerations. First, God has clearly informed us that He has eternally elected a certain number of sinners and that He has reprobated others and determined to leave them to go on in their sins. Christ alludes to this deep doctrine when He says to the unbelieving Jews: "Ye believe not, because ye are not of my sheep, as I said unto you. My sheep hear my voice, and I know them, and they follow me: and I give unto them eternal life" (John 10:26–28).

The second dimension of the mystery of God's sincere offer of the gospel lies in the clearly revealed fact that faith is something that the sinner cannot exercise of himself. The sinner ought to obey the call of the gospel, but of himself he cannot do so. In other words, faith is the sinner's duty, but it is a duty he cannot possibly perform. For without the grace of God, no man can come to Christ. Jesus Himself teaches this: "No man can come to me, except the Father which hath sent me draw him" (John 6:44). Why can't the sinner believe by his own willpower? It is because the sinner's willpower is in bondage to sin. So there are two aspects to the mystery of the free offer of the gospel: How can God require the sinner to believe when he is incapable of exercising faith?

Further, how can God sincerely offer the salvation of the gospel to all men when He has eternally decreed that not all will be saved? Let us look at each problem individually.

God has every right to require a sinner to do what He gave us all power to do originally at our creation. As God created us, we were capable of believing every word of God and of carrying out every duty. The fact that we cannot now obey God's commands because we are sinful is entirely our fault. God has every right to command us to do what He gave us power to do in our original state of perfection. So when the gospel comes to a sinner, God has every right to require him to believe it. Faith is a man's duty even though it is a duty that of himself he cannot perform.

Furthermore, if a sinner humbles himself before God and cries out for grace to be given to do what he cannot do on his own, God will be merciful to him. This was precisely the case with the father of the demon-possessed child when he cried out to Christ, "Lord, I believe; help thou mine unbelief" (Mark 9:24). He immediately received the help of Christ. And so will all who cry out sincerely to God for His mercy and help.

The second aspect of the mystery is this: How can God be said to offer a sincere pardon to those whom He has eternally reprobated? The number of the elect is fixed in eternity past. Their number will neither increase nor diminish. God well knows who the elect are. Then isn't it misleading to say that God gives a sincere offer of mercy to those who are not His elect?

There are two incorrect ways of addressing this mystery. One mistake is to deny election and to say that the sinner has the power of free will to believe in Christ of himself. This is to contradict the Word of God, which clearly states that believers are "chosen" in Christ "before the foundation of the world" (Eph. 1:4). Nothing can be clearer than the truth that Christians come to salvation because they were chosen by Christ. Jesus' own words are "Ye have not chosen me, but I have chosen you" (John 15:16).

The alternative mistake is to suppose that the gospel is not sincerely offered to *all* who hear it but only to the elect. However, this is not scriptural either. It is God's revealed will that all who hear the message should believe it. It is the preacher's duty to invite *all* to come, and it is the duty of *all* who hear the gospel to comply with God's gracious invitation. God has "no pleasure in the death of the wicked; but that the wicked turn from his way and live" (Ezek. 33:11). The Scriptures make it plain that God "will have all men to be saved, and to come unto the knowledge of the truth" (1 Tim. 2:4). The Scriptures tell us that "the Lord is not slack concerning his promise, as some men count slackness; but is longsuffering to us-ward, not willing that any should perish, but that all should come to repentance" (2 Peter 3:9).

Here we face a mystery in connection with the gospel. God informs us that He wishes all men to come to repentance and faith but that He has not elected them all to come. God sincerely invites and summons all who hear the gospel to come, but He has not chosen them all. What are we to think in light of these biblical teachings?

We are to realize that here we face a mystery that we cannot fully explain in this life. When we come face-to-face with questions involving the sovereignty of God it behooves us to put our hand on our mouth, as Paul tells us: "Nay but, O man, who art thou that repliest against God? Shall the thing formed say to him that formed it, Why hast thou made me thus? Hath not the potter power over the clay, of the same lump to make one vessel unto honour, and another unto dishonour?" (Rom. 9:20–21).

It is clear that God is good. He has made full and perfect provision for sinners in the finished work of Christ. In so doing, God has manifested His amazingly great love to the world. God invites all to believe and be saved. Yet God is Lord of all His creatures. He has exercised His lordship in that He has chosen some, but not all, to salvation. Without His grace none can believe in Christ, yet we remember that God is under no obligation to give saving grace to any man. The sinner who truly wishes to be saved by Christ will be saved. Those who reject the gospel are accountable for their rejection of it. Their blood will be on their own head. In the day of judgment, if they heard the gospel and rejected it, they cannot say they were not invited.

The mystery we have considered here should have an effect upon us. It should make us deeply grateful that we live in days when the gospel is preached to all men, and all are bidden to come. Further, the mystery of the gospel and its presentation in the light of God's sovereignty should stir us up to seek to be more fruitful in our preaching and in our witnessing to the unsaved. Mysteries belong to God; duty belongs to us. The world is full of precious souls needing to hear the gospel of God's love. May our consideration of these deep things of God move us to plead with God to give us all more gospel power.

Christ told the Pharisees that they were not His sheep (John 10:26). Nonetheless, when He saw the cloud of God's judgment that hung over Jerusalem, He did not dispassionately shrug His shoulders. On the contrary, He "beheld the city, and wept over it" (Luke 19:41). Our duty as Christ's people is clear enough: "Go ye into all the world, and preach the gospel to every creature. He that believeth and is baptized shall be saved; but he that believeth not shall be damned" (Mark 16:15–16).

9

The Mystery of the Gentiles

The mystery...that the Gentiles should be fel-
low heirs, and of the same body, and partakers
of his promise in Christ by the gospel.

—EPHESIANS 3:3–6

God saw fit early in the history of the world to make the nation of Israel (the Jews) different from all other nations. This important separation began with God's call to Abraham and His promise that "in thee [Abraham] shall all families of the earth be blessed" (Gen. 12:3). God gave the people of Israel religious privileges, as well as privileges of other kinds, which at that date were not given to the other nations on the earth. The apostle Paul summarizes Israel's privileges with these words: "Who are Israelites; to whom pertaineth the adoption, and the glory, and the covenants, and the giving of the law, and the service of God, and the promises; whose are the fathers, and of whom as concerning the flesh Christ came, who is over all, God blessed for ever. Amen" (Rom. 9:4–5).

God made this separation of the Jews a matter of fact and also of duty. They were to maintain their distinct and separate character, especially in the observance of God's worship and in the laws and regulations, provisions, and punishments God revealed to them through Moses and the prophets. At the heart of this separation was the extremely important principle that Israel alone worshiped the true God and kept the divinely ordained forms of worship. As the tragic consequence of sin, all other nations had lapsed to a greater or lesser degree into idolatry, paganism, and unbelief.

Israel's covenanted duty to God was to observe His worship and service carefully by adhering to His revealed will in the Old Testament Scriptures. When they did so, they received God's blessing. But when they were careless and disobedient, as was the case all too often, they suffered God's judgments. These took the form of wars, diseases, and famines, to name a few. The historical books of the Old Testament are an inspired record of Israel's rise and fall time and again, depending on whether they kept to God's law or backslid into the pagan practices of the surrounding nations.

In Old Testament times, therefore, the only nation on earth that had the true God, the true gospel, and the hope of salvation was the Jewish nation. All other nations and civilizations, whether cultured like Greece and Rome or uncultured like most others, lived in spiritual darkness and under the wrath of God. In those Old Testament days, only Israel among all the nations on earth was favored with the true religion that God revealed to them by His inspired messengers, like Moses and Isaiah.

Scripture clearly proves this to be true. At Sinai, God says to Moses in reference to Israel, "If ye will obey my voice indeed, and keep my covenant, then ye shall be a peculiar treasure unto me above all people: for all the earth is mine" (Ex. 19:5). This is echoed by the psalmist: "For the LORD hath chosen Jacob unto himself, and Israel for his peculiar treasure" (Ps. 135:4). Again, the prophet Amos says, "You only have I known of all the families of the earth" (Amos 3:2). To the same effect, the Lord Jesus Christ says to the woman of Samaria, "Salvation is of the Jews" (John 4:22).

Scripture demonstrates that in Old Testament times, Israel alone had the knowledge of the true God. No other nations received the privileges of true religion. They lived and perished in their sins. The only exceptions were Gentile men and women who, by one means or other, came to know the true God through contact with Jews. Such persons included Rahab, Ruth, Naaman, and certain inhabitants of Nineveh in the days of Jonah, together with the converts to Judaism who were called proselytes.

It must be understood that while all Jews had great religious privileges in the days before Christ, not all were saved. There were, in those times, Jews who were converted and Jews who were not converted.

Paul expresses this in these words: "They are not all Israel, which are of Israel: neither, because they are the seed of Abraham, are they all children.... They which are the children of the flesh, these are not the children of God: but the children of the promise are counted for the seed" (Rom. 9:6–8). This is such an important fact that Paul, in another place, states, "He is not a Jew, which is one outwardly; neither is that circumcision, which is outward in the flesh: but he is a Jew, which is one inwardly; and circumcision is that of the heart" (Rom. 2:28–29).

We must be very clear on this point. In Old Testament times all Jews were highly privileged in that before the coming of Christ, God sovereignly chose to give to that nation only the true way of worship and salvation. But, just as in other nations today that are favored with gospel privileges, not all believed. Believing Jews, who had saving grace, lived and died well and so went to glory. Hebrews 11 records some of their names.

But very many Jews died in unbelief and, sadly, have gone to eternal punishment in hell. Let no one suppose that all Jews—because they were Jews—went to heaven in pre-Christian times. Only those Jews who believed God's Word were saved. They needed to be born again of God's Holy Spirit and justified by faith in precisely the same way in which New Testament believers are saved today.

What then is the mystery that the apostle Paul refers to in his reference to the Gentiles, or non-Jewish people, of the world (Eph. 3:1–6)? It is that, after the coming of Christ, God threw open the door of salvation to *all* nations, Gentile as well as Jewish.

This great alteration in God's dealings with mankind began with the day of Pentecost when the Holy Spirit came upon the men and they "began to speak with other tongues, as the Spirit gave them utterance" (Acts 2:4). Tongues, or languages, are the vehicle of expression of the different nations and tribes of the world. Whereas before Pentecost truth and salvation were associated with the languages used by the Jews, now *all* nations were invited to partake of God's gracious salvation. This wonderful change in God's dealings with mankind came as a shock to the crowd at Jerusalem: "How hear we every man in our own tongue, wherein we were born?" (Acts 2:8). They even give a list of the national languages that they heard being spoken by the apostles. These evidently included some languages from countries to the east of Judea, as well as Egyptian, Latin, Greek, and Arabic (see Acts 2:9–11).

A new day had dawned on mankind when the Spirit came down at Pentecost. Even the apostles themselves did not fully appreciate how great and important the change was for some time. This is clear from the account we have of the vision given to Peter of a vessel descending from heaven in which "were all manner of fourfooted beasts of the earth, and wild beasts, and creeping things, and fowls of the air" (Acts 10:12). To explain the vision a voice came to Peter from heaven: "What God hath cleansed, that call not thou common" (Acts 10:15). In a word, *all* nations are now called on by God to enter His kingdom. No longer is God's grace confined to the Jews or to those who become disciples of the Jewish religion.

To give expression to his amazement, Peter exclaimed before his Gentile audience, "Of a truth I perceive that God is no respecter of persons: But in every nation he that feareth him, and worketh righteousness, is accepted with him" (Acts 10:34–35). As a full and unanswerable sign that this was now so, the Holy Spirit came, after Peter had offered the gospel to them, upon the Gentile hearers: "The Holy Ghost fell on all them which heard the word. And they of the circumcision which believed were astonished…because that on the Gentiles also was poured out the gift of the Holy Ghost" (Acts 10:44–45).

In the wisdom of God, the apostle Paul was especially ordained by Him to bring the gospel of Christ to the Gentile world. Paul himself was aware of this distinct calling. He informs us that he received a "revelation" (Eph. 3:3) from God to make it known to him that his special task in the ministry was to bring Christ's gospel to the Gentile world: "Unto me, who am less than the least of all saints, is this grace given, that I should preach among the Gentiles the unsearchable riches of Christ" (Eph. 3:8).

It is, perhaps, difficult for us today, after some two thousand years of Gentile evangelism, to realize that this opening of the door of faith to non-Jews was, at the time of Pentecost, an unexpected event in the Jewish world. Many Jews resented the very thought of God's grace extending beyond Israel. When Paul addressed the excited Jewish crowd in Jerusalem to explain his conversion and ministry, they listened until he informed them of his sense of divine calling to preach to the Gentiles. At that point a riot broke out: "They gave him audience unto this word, and then lifted up their voices, and said, Away with such a fellow from the earth: for it is not fit that he should live" (Acts 22:22). Sadly, the Jews at that date were reluctant to allow any other nation into the blessings of the covenant.

What the Jews of Paul's day evidently overlooked and became blind to was that in various Scriptures from the Old Testament, God had stated that the Gentiles would one day be blessed in Christ. For example, God said to Abraham, "In thee shall all families of the earth be blessed" (Gen. 12:3). The Psalms refer to the spread of the gospel in several places. Psalm 22 says, "All the ends of the world shall remember and turn unto the LORD" (v. 27). In another psalm we read, "He shall have dominion also from sea to sea" (72:8). Isaiah declares: "He shall bring forth judgment to the Gentiles" (42:1). Indeed, Isaiah prophesies the casting off of the Jews and the calling of the Gentiles. It is with this solemn message that his prophecy concludes (see Isaiah 66). However, these prophecies were not appreciated by the bulk of the Jewish nation in the time of Christ and the apostles. Jewish exclusivism had closed their own eyes to the glorious fact that one day the Word of God would extend to all nations. This day of Gentile grace dawned at Pentecost.

The "mystery of the Gentiles," then, is this wonderful fact that God has, since Pentecost, opened up the door of His grace to all nations. At the same time, very sadly, the Jews became hardened. They rejected Jesus as their Messiah and so placed themselves under God's wrath. For the past two thousand years they have been cut off from the saving grace of God. As Paul says, "Because of unbelief they were broken off" (Rom. 11:20). As Paul makes clear, the day will come when Israel will be brought back into the church. Meanwhile, they are in a state of exclusion through unbelief.

How long will the time of Israel's exclusion last? Christ explains this point in these words: "Jerusalem shall be trodden down of the Gentiles, until the times of the Gentiles be fulfilled" (Luke 21:24). At some point in the future God will bless Israel again as a nation. The Jews will be favored with a religious revival that will mark the end of their apostasy. Paul makes the following prophecy: "Blindness in part is happened to Israel, until the fulness of the Gentiles be come in" (Rom. 11:25).

Our duty as Gentile believers in the meantime is to love the Jewish people and to show them every kindness. Further, we should pray daily that God would hasten the time of their "ingrafting" (Rom. 11:23) into the church of Christ. As Gentiles, may we never lose sight of the fact that Israel lost the favor of God by their rejection of Christ and His gospel. Their unbelief is a warning to us today. "Be not highminded, but fear: for if God spared not the natural branches, take heed lest he also spare not thee" (Rom. 11:20–21). This apostolic warning is surely relevant to Gentile churches at this hour!

10

The Mystery of Israel

For I would not, brethren, that ye should be ignorant of this mystery, lest ye should be wise in your own conceits; that blindness in part is happened to Israel, until the fulness of the Gentiles be come in. And so all Israel shall be saved.

— ROMANS 11:25

The mystery revealed in Romans 11:25 is that the Jewish people, who have been blind to Christ's gospel now for some two thousand years, will one day be brought back into the church. This will take place as the result of a revival. The Deliverer will come to open their eyes to allow them to recognize Jesus Christ as their Messiah. This Deliverer is the Holy Spirit who, as Paul states here when quoting from Isaiah, will illuminate the truth of the gospel to the Jewish people (Isa. 59:20–21). It is a revival of religion that will fulfill God's covenant promise to be a God to them and to their seed forever (Jer. 31:35–37).

The calling of the Gentiles two thousand years ago was a mystery, and it took the Jews by surprise at the time. They stumbled over Christ and fell into unbelief. But they will not be left in that condition forever. Paul, in Romans 11, explains these two points clearly. The Jews fell away from God after the coming of Christ, and the cause of this was their unbelief: "Because of unbelief they were broken off" (Rom. 11:20). But we are not to suppose that Israel has fallen into apostasy forever. "They also," argues Paul, "if they abide not still in unbelief, shall be grafted in, for God is able to graft them in again" (Rom. 11:23).

Paul makes two things clear in this most interesting chapter. First, the Gentiles have been brought into the church of God in these New Testament times, and the Jews have, for a time, been largely cast out through unbelief. But secondly, the Jews will at some point in the future be brought back into the church and enjoy the blessings of the gospel.

The apostle uses an illustration in Romans 11. He compares the church of God to a cultivated olive tree (vv. 16–24) and the Gentile world to a wild olive tree (v. 24). The Jewish nation, descending from Abraham and the other patriarchs, stands in a special relationship to God. They are the "natural branches" (v. 24), whereas the Gentile world, not having descent from the Old Testament saints, is a "wild olive tree" (v. 17).

When Gentiles come to faith in Christ, as they have done now for some two thousand years since Pentecost, they are comparable to branches cut out of a wild olive tree and grafted into the cultivated olive tree (v. 17). On the other hand, when Jewish persons reject the gospel of Christ, as for some two thousand years the majority of them have done, they are to be looked on as branches that are "broken off" (vv. 19–20).

The tree is the church. It is alive and growing. In Abraham's time there was but a root. In Old Testament times the branches were almost exclusively Jewish. Very few Gentiles were saved in the days before Christ. But at Pentecost a dramatic alteration came about. God turned to the Gentiles and very largely turned His back on the Jews (Acts 28:24–28). This was a divine judgment on them for rejecting Christ. God gave them what they asked for when they cried out against Christ, "His blood be on us, and on our children" (Matt. 27:25). Since Pentecost, God has been engrafting Gentiles from all nations into the church.

We must not miss the point when Paul declares in this chapter, "And so all Israel shall be saved" (Rom. 11:26). He is not simply telling us that all God's elect will be saved, as true and encouraging as this is. But Paul is here explaining the mystery that he has just referred to, namely that the Jews as a body will be brought into the church again at some time in the future. The proof that this is his meaning is evident in the language he uses: "And they also, if they abide not still in unbelief, shall be grafted in: for God is able to graft them in again" (Rom. 11:23).

Difficulties in the interpretation of Paul's words in Romans 11 must be cleared away when we focus our attention on these words: "God is able to graft them in again" (v. 23). These words are crucial to the recognition of the mystery in Romans 11. To "graft them in again" implies three things: (1) they were in at one time; (2) they are not in now; (3) they are capable of being grafted in again by God's power.

There is only one nation on earth that fits this condition—the Jews, who *were* God's people in Old Testament times but who fell into apostasy through their rejection of Christ and have been, apart from a few in every age, outside the Christian church since the times of the apostles. The mystery, therefore, is that they will at some point in the future be spiritually revived again and brought into the church. But in the meantime they are, sad to say, in a condition of unbelief.

We are given a key for understanding God's gracious plan in the salvation of mankind. It is in three stages: (1) in Old Testament times the Jews were saved, but very few Gentiles were saved; (2) now in this present age, since Pentecost, it is mostly Gentiles who are saved but very few Jews; (3) and finally, before the end of time, both Jews and Gentiles will be saved.

It seems clear that Christ alludes to this aspect of God's plan of salvation when He says: "Jerusalem shall be trodden down of the Gentiles, until the times of the Gentiles be fulfilled" (Luke 21:24). The expression "the times of the Gentiles" would seem to be a reference to the second period of God's saving dealings with mankind. In other words, a time is yet to come in God's providence in which He will no longer give the grace of His gospel mainly to Gentiles. When that day comes in which "the times of the Gentiles" are fulfilled, God will again open the door of faith to Israel.

Great numbers of Jews will then understand that Jesus was their Messiah after all. The prophet Zechariah surely refers to this blessed day when he declares in the name of Christ: "I will pour upon the house of David, and upon the inhabitants of Jerusalem, the spirit of grace and of supplications: and they shall look upon me whom they have pierced, and they shall mourn for him, as one mourneth for his only son.... In that day there shall be a fountain opened to the house of David and to the inhabitants of Jerusalem for sin and for uncleanness" (Zech. 12:10; 13:1).

Jews everywhere will, by faith in the gospel, recognize Christ when this happens. They will weep and sorrow deeply that their forefathers were so blind that they did not recognize Christ as their Messiah when He first came. And they will find forgiveness in the blood that Jesus shed for sinners—for Jews as well as for all other nations. The prophet depicts this revival of the Jews in very moving language: "There [shall] be a great mourning in Jerusalem" (Zech. 12:11).

The Lord Jesus Christ also surely alludes to this restoration of Israel when He says to the Jews as a nation: "Behold, your house is left unto you desolate. For I say unto you, ye shall not see me henceforth, till ye shall say, blessed is he that cometh in the name of the Lord" (Matt. 23:38–39). In other words, our Lord is announcing that, because of their unbelief, the Holy Spirit will be withdrawn from them, and they will become spiritually dead for a long period of time as a consequence. But this will not last forever. A future day will come when the Spirit of enlightenment will graciously be restored to them. In that day they will bless God because He has visited them in grace once more. The Spirit who will come upon them will enable them to see Christ in their own Scriptures, the Christ whom they have failed to see all these years.

It is clear that long ago God revealed Christ and the crucifixion to the Jews (for example, Isa. 53; Ps. 22; Ps. 69; Zech. 13:7). But they have not understood their own Scriptures because a veil is over their eyes. The future restoration of the Spirit to Israel will result in their eyes being opened to see Christ clearly. The apostle Paul, in another of his epistles, informs us that this veil of blindness will one day be removed: "For until this day remaineth the same veil untaken away in the reading of the old testament; which veil is done away in Christ. But even unto this day, when Moses is read, the veil is upon their heart. Nevertheless when it shall turn to the Lord, the veil shall be taken away" (2 Cor. 3:14–16).

All these Scriptures, therefore, shed light upon the mystery concerning Israel's future restoration and re-engrafting into the church of God. But what effect will this event have on the Gentiles? It will have the wonderful effect of reviving them and so bringing still more blessing upon mankind, as Paul says, "If the fall of them be the riches of the world, and the diminishing of them the riches of the Gentiles; how much more their fulness?" (Rom. 11:12). Again, he says, "For if the casting away of them be the reconciling of the world, what shall the receiving of them be, but life from the dead?" (Rom. 11:15).

May God hasten this blessed day in which Jews and Gentiles will both enjoy this "life from the dead"!

11

The Mystery of Iniquity

For the mystery of iniquity doth already work.
—2 THESSALONIANS 2:7

The "mystery of iniquity" has been revealed to Christians as a warning, to put us on our guard against error and superstition. God is a God of truth. He requires that we worship Him "in spirit and in truth" (John 4:23). He has revealed the truth to us in holy Scripture and has given us the warning that "though…an angel from heaven, preach any other gospel" to us than that revealed to us through the apostles in the Bible, we must "let him be accursed" (Gal. 1:8). The effect of truth is to enlighten the mind and sanctify the soul. The effect of error in doctrine and practice is to blind men so that they fall into "the ditch" of hell (Matt. 15:14).

God reveals this mystery of iniquity to us in order to make us aware of a most serious and harmful form of error which we must expect to meet in this life. That God so warns us is a much-needed reminder that we have powerful and subtle enemies against us, enemies who would drag us down to eternal perdition if they could. Our duty, therefore, is to seek to understand this dark mystery and to pray for grace to avoid it.

In seeking to interpret this mystery of iniquity it is essential to have the exact words of the apostle Paul before us. These words are found in 2 Thessalonians 2:1–12:

> Now we beseech you, brethren, by the coming of our Lord Jesus Christ, and by our gathering together unto him, That ye be not soon shaken in mind, or be troubled, neither by spirit, nor by word, nor by letter as from us, as that the day of Christ is at hand. Let no man deceive you by any means: for that day shall not come, except there come a falling away first, and that man of sin be revealed, the son of perdition; who opposeth and exalteth himself above all that is called God, or that is worshipped; so that he as God sitteth in the temple of God, showing himself that he is God. Remember ye not, that, when I was yet with you, I told you these things? And now ye know what withholdeth that he might be revealed in his time. For the mystery of iniquity doth already work: only he who now letteth will let, until he be taken out of the way. And then shall that Wicked be revealed, whom the Lord shall consume with the spirit of his mouth, and shall destroy with the brightness of his coming: even him, whose coming is after the working of Satan with all power and signs and lying wonders, and with

all deceivableness of unrighteousness in them
that perish; because they received not the love
of the truth, that they might be saved. And for
this cause God shall send them strong delusion,
that they should believe a lie: that they all might
be damned who believed not the truth, but had
pleasure in unrighteousness.

It is clear on first reading these words that they refer
to an evil force of immense wickedness. It is no ordi-
nary person who "opposeth and exalteth himself
above all that is called God, or that is worshipped."
It is obvious that this mystery of iniquity relates to
a figure of extreme arrogance in that he "sitteth in
the temple of God, showing himself that he is God"
(v. 4). We meet with sin all around us in this life,
but the figure of evil revealed to us in this mystery is
clearly a person of extraordinary wickedness, for his
"coming is after the working of Satan with all power
and signs and lying wonders" (v. 9).

To identify this mystery of iniquity we need to
look at the clue Paul gives us here: "And now ye
know what withholdeth that he might be revealed in
his time" (v. 6). This statement means that this mystery had not yet become visible. There was a power
at work in the apostle's day that was "withholding,"
or keeping back, the mystery. However, when this
restraining power would be "taken out of the way"
(v. 7), the mystery would be visible for all to see.

There is no mistaking what this restraining
power was in Paul's day: the Roman Empire. So long

as Rome's mighty civil power existed it would not be possible for the mystery of iniquity to emerge visibly. It is important to know that learned Christian writers in the early church also identified the restraining power here as the Roman Empire. These church fathers were Tertullian and Irenaeus, both of whom lived in the century after the apostle Paul.

Since the identification of pagan Rome as the restraining force mentioned here is so important, we need to realize that other church fathers who lived in later centuries took the same view. These words of the learned church father Jerome, who translated the Scriptures into the Latin text that we call the Vulgate, are especially worth noting: "Let us therefore say, what all Ecclesiastical Writers have delivered to us, that when the Roman Empire is to be destroyed...then will be revealed the Man of Sin, the Son of Perdition, who will venture to take his seat in the Temple of God, making himself as God" (*Commentary on Daniel 7*, 3:1101). Why didn't Paul simply say that the restraining power was the Roman Empire? The answer is because the Roman authorities of his day would have been displeased. They thought of the Roman Empire as eternal. They imagined that Rome would last forever. Had Paul named Rome as a power that would one day end, he would have brought needless persecution on early Christians from the Roman civil authorities. Hence Paul uses very guarded language when he refers to a time when the Roman Empire would be at an end.

Who then is the man of sin referred to here by Paul? The answer we give must take into account several important factors referred to prophetically by Paul in this epistle. These factors are as follows:

1. There is to be a "falling away" in the Christian church (v. 3).

2. This man of sin is a rival of Almighty God (v. 4).

3. This evil phenomenon will exist for hundreds of years, right up until the second coming of Christ Himself (v. 8).

4. He will have power to do miracles, whether true or false (v. 9).

5. His coming is a judgment on those who do not love the genuine gospel of God (v. 10).

6. He represents a spurious, lying version of God's religion (v. 11).

7. Those who believe his lie will lose their soul (v. 12).

What Paul tells us here leads us to draw up some guidelines to assist in the identification of this mystery of iniquity. First, the man of sin will not introduce what is obviously a non-Christian religion. He will be the promoter of a perverted form of Christ's religion. He will make astounding and blasphemous claims for himself—claims which amount to Godhood (v. 4). He will not be a single individual but a series of men holding office as heads of Christ's church. His appeal will be to pseudo-Christians who have no love for the real truths of Christianity. Finally, he will begin to show himself on the stage of history once the Roman Empire collapses.

How do we, in light of the above, draw conclusions about the identity of this man of sin? The following facts of history must be kept in mind. The city of Rome was sacked by Alaric, king of the German Visigoths, in AD 410. The last Roman emperor who ruled in the Western Empire was Romulus Augustulus, who died in AD 476. The Western Empire of Rome was then totally extinct, and the rule of Italy was taken over by the barbarian King Odoacer, who reigned until AD 490. The scene was now set for the appearing of the man of sin. The restraining power was gone. Who now rose up with the pretensions and claims prophesied by Paul?

There can only be one answer: the papacy. Over the centuries, the popes of Rome have laid claim to extraordinary importance in the church of Christ and over the affairs of mankind. Around AD 600, the bishop of Rome began to advance the claim that he was the universal bishop of the entire Christian church. In process of time, popes laid claim to still greater and greater power. It was this fact that led Wycliffe, Luther, Calvin, and the Westminster divines to interpret this passage of Scripture as a prophecy of the rise and progress of the Antichrist.

It is important to note that when our Protestant forefathers described the papacy as the Antichrist they were not indulging in the weakness of men who criticize their adversaries with abusive language. Their identification of the popes as the individuals who literally fulfill the apostle's prophecy in 2 Thessalonians 2:1–12 has the full support of history. Moreover, the papal claims, which over many centuries have grown greater and greater, fully justify Protestants in identifying the mystery of iniquity as the papacy and, therefore, inevitably include the Roman Catholic system of religion under that label as well.

The history of the popes makes it very clear that their claims far exceed what is proper for any mere human being to make. Whereas the apostle Peter describes himself simply as "a servant and an apostle of Jesus Christ" (2 Peter 1:1), and again as "also an elder, and a witness of the sufferings of Christ" (1 Peter 5:1), the popes lay claim to superhuman authority and allow themselves to be addressed with this kind of language: "Receive the tiara adorned with three crowns and know that thou art Father of princes and kings, Ruler of the world, Vicar of our Savior Jesus Christ."[1]

A detailed description of Roman Catholic dogma, miracles, Mary worship, and persecution of God's dear people over the centuries is beyond our present scope. But enough has been said to remind us that we must not, as some in our day want to do, go soft on the evils of papal religion.

---

1. During a pope's coronation, a tiara is placed on his head, accompanied by these words. As cited in Paul Hutchinson and Winifred E. Garrison, *20 Centuries of Christianity* (New York: Harcourt, Brace, 1959),120.

12

The Mystery of the Last Things

But in the days of the voice of the seventh angel, when he shall begin to sound, the mystery of God should be finished, as he hath declared to his servants the prophets.
—REVELATION 10:7

As we have seen, a mystery is an event in the purposes of God that we cannot know about unless God has graciously revealed it to us in the Bible. The history of the world will end with four great mysteries that we do well to study and seek to understand insofar as the Bible tells us about them. These mysteries are the resurrection of the body, the day of judgment, heaven, and hell. When history ends—and it will end—with these four mighty things, the plan of God for His creatures will be complete. The mystery of God will be finished.

Before explicating these four last things we need to remind ourselves of what is preliminary to them all: physical death. There are three forms of death: physical death, spiritual death, and eternal death. The common feature of all three is a form of separation. In physical, or temporal, death the soul is separated from the body in which it was housed here on earth. The body returns to dust, from which it was originally taken when God created man (Gen. 2:7). At the point of physical death the soul (or spirit of man) enters at once into eternity. In spiritual death, which is the condition of every sinner in this life prior to the new birth, the soul is in a state of separation from God and therefore is dead to the truths revealed in the Bible. In eternal death, which will occur in the experience of every nonbeliever after the last judgment, both body and soul will be separated from God eternally.

Our concern in this discussion is with temporal death—that is, when God summons the soul of any man or woman to leave this life and to appear before Him in the eternity beyond this world. Everyone, apart from Enoch, Elijah, and those alive when Christ returns at the end of the world, must die this physical death. The condition of man's soul at death will determine whether he enters into happiness or misery. We refer to this state in which the soul is disembodied and lives separate from the body in another place as the intermediate state.

The souls of believers in this intermediate state are immediately made holy and happy. They are beyond the reach of sin, sorrow, and fear. They are "with Christ; which is far better" (Phil. 1:23). However, though perfectly blessed, the soul is incomplete in that it still awaits its own body. Christ, by His death, purchased the soul and also the body of His people. In the intermediate state, therefore, the believer is in a state of happiness with Christ, but he still awaits the last trumpet, when his body will be restored to him.

The condition of the unbeliever's soul at death will be, alas, one of misery and profound suffering. He will be subjected to the judgments of God for all his sins done on earth. Along with this agony he will have the fearful realization that there is now no hope of being saved. His torments will continue until the end of the world, when his body will be raised up in the general resurrection. After that he must experience God's wrath and curse eternally in hellfire, both in soul and body. This is unquestionably a most serious subject. The Bible speaks about it very clearly and frequently.

No one refers to this awesome theme more frequently than Jesus Christ, who came to save us from such a fearful eternity. Out of love for us, He tells us of this place of punishment so that we might flee to Him for pardon and cleansing. We will deal with the subject of the resurrection of the body in chapter 13, so let us now turn to look at the subject of the day of judgment.

It is one of the sad follies of mankind that, although the Bible speaks so often of this day of judgment, few take the necessary steps to prepare for it. This fact in itself is further evidence of the divine inspiration of the Bible. For our Savior tells us that when the last day comes, men will be utterly and entirely unprepared: "And as it was in the days of Noah, so shall it be also in the days of the Son of Man. They did eat, they drank, they married wives, they were given in marriage, until the day that Noah entered into the ark, and the flood came, and destroyed them all" (Luke 17:26–27). Christ says this was the case of proud and godless Sodom, which was consumed by "fire and brimstone" from heaven (Luke 17:29). Our Lord then applies this to society as it will be at the end of the world: "Even thus shall it be in the day when the Son of man is revealed" (Luke 17:30). The message is clear: Be forewarned! Be prepared! But, alas, few listen.

The day of judgment has been appointed by God for very good and necessary reasons. In this present life God has left many things unfinished. Good men often die under a cloud of false accusations that many choose to believe. On the other hand, evil men and hypocrites often die with the reputation of heroes. The unrighteous are praised and the righteous are scolded. They who have loved and served God faithfully may die in obscurity, unknown and without reward. The godless, on the other hand, may go famous to the grave and enjoy a reputation of honor for generations afterwards.

All such inequalities must be put right in the end. God's justice requires that in the great day of judgment every person must be shown publicly to the entire universe to be what he really is in the estimation of God. So in that day there will be a resurrection of reputations as well as of bodies. God's estimation of every individual man and woman will be made public in that great day.

The judge will be the Lord Jesus Christ Himself. The authority to pass sentence upon all has been given by God to His Son, the God-man (John 5:27). This is most appropriate. Christ has been rejected by the world; He will finally pass judgment on the world. He is God, and therefore He is perfectly just and accurate in His evaluation of men and of their motives and actions.

He is also human. No one will be able to accuse Christ of being ignorant of the trials and tribulations of this world. Like others, Jesus has been through this life and knows what a difficult place the world is. His judgment will proceed on the basis of perfect knowledge of all men and perfect knowledge of all the circumstances that men have had to go through in this world. The Lord Jesus is the ideal and perfect Judge. No man can appeal the sentence that He will pass. "Every mouth [will] be stopped" (Rom. 3:19), and all the world will know itself to be deserving of the sentence that Jesus Christ will pass on each person individually.

There can be only two kinds of verdicts. The righteous will be welcomed to glory and to heaven. Their sins will, for Christ's sake, all be pardoned. The unrighteous will be commanded to depart from Christ as those who, being condemned for their sins, must now enter "into everlasting fire, prepared for the devil and his angels" (Matt. 25:41).

The righteousness of the righteous in that day consists of the righteousness of Christ, imputed to them in the moment of their believing His gospel. All sins of the righteous are pardoned because they are washed and cleansed in the blood of Christ. Their reward will be in proportion to their deeds of service and love done in this life for Christ.

The guilt of the wicked will include not only their acts of disobedience to God's revealed will but also their sins of omission, in that they did not in this life show love for Christ by ministering to His dear people in their time of need (Matt. 25:42–45). The degree of punishment will be suited to the measure of the evil which every godless person has done in this life.

In addition, account will be taken by the Judge of the measure of religious knowledge which each person had here in the world. Those who sinned against greater light will be "beaten with many stripes," and those who sinned against lesser light will be "beaten with few stripes" (Luke 12:47–48). Hence, "it shall be more tolerable for the land of Sodom in the day of judgment" (Matt. 11:24) than for those who have lived in lands where there are Bibles, churches, and Christian books in plenty.

The day of judgment will be followed at once by the final state: heaven and hell. Christ will renew the universe by His power so that there will then be "new heavens and a new earth, wherein dwelleth righteousness" (2 Peter 3:13). There will no longer be a state of probation as there now is in this present world. Once the day of judgment is past, every one of us will have a character which, either good or evil, will be ours unchangeably and forever: "He that is unjust, let him be unjust still…he that is righteous, let him be righteous still" (Rev. 22:11). There is no purgatory. The gospel is no more. Time is up for every man and woman. The obvious and supremely important lesson from these mysteries is: "Repent ye, and believe the gospel" (Mark 1:15).

13

The Mystery of
the Resurrection

*Behold, I show you a mystery; we shall not all
sleep, but we shall all be changed.*

—1 CORINTHIANS 15:51

The words of the famous text above refer to the mystery of the act of glorification which is to take place at the end of the world. It is a thing we could never have known if God had not graciously revealed it to us in His Word. The act of glorification will occur in the human body of every Christian at the end of the world. The wonderful encouragement given here to every believer is that when the last day eventually comes, the body in which we now live will be divinely changed so that it will no longer appear as it does now, but we will have a new and far superior appearance.

The condition and appearance of the body can be altered in different ways. As we grow older, our bodies undergo visible alteration. We may think of this as physical decline brought about by the normal aging process. At age seventy we are not as good-looking as we were at age twenty. As the body ages, it loses some of its beauty and luster. The reason for this is that because we are sinful, death is gradually creeping up on us all.

When we die, our bodies begin to decay and return to the dust. This fulfills God's word of judgment on Adam after he sinned: "Dust thou art, and unto dust shalt thou return" (Gen. 3:19). In a state of death the body disintegrates and becomes just a quantity of dust. This has happened all throughout history and will continue to do so until the end of time.

The only exception is the human body of Christ, who had no sin. Christ's body in the grave did not begin to decompose. This was a unique favor conferred on Him by God the Father as part of His reward for obedience to the Father's will. We know this to be so from Scripture (Ps. 16:10; Acts 2:27).

When a believer dies, therefore, his or her soul goes at once to glory to be with Christ. It is immediately made perfect in holiness and is full of joy in the presence of the Lord. But this condition is not to last forever. Christ has not only purchased the salvation of our souls by His death, He has also procured the redemption of our bodies as well. Therefore, when the last day comes, the bodies and souls of believers who have died will be reunited. If we are Christians, we will rise from the dead in glory—perfect both in soul and in body.

What will happen in the last day to Christians who are still alive on earth? They, like the Christians who have died, will be changed. That is to say, their bodies will be glorified and their souls will be made perfect in the same moment. So all Christians who have died will be raised up in a worldwide resurrection and made fit for heaven. And at exactly the same time, all Christians who have not died will be glorified by an act of God.

God has revealed to us that these events will take place in a particular order. Those Christians who have died and are raised up on the last day will ascend first to meet Christ. Then those Christians who have not died but who have been transformed instantaneously upon Christ's return will be "caught up together" (1 Thess. 4:17) with resurrected believers. So both groups of Christians, those resurrected and those who never died, will "be caught up together with them in the clouds, to meet the Lord in the air" (1 Thess. 4:17). Evidently, believers who have experienced death will be given priority in meeting the Lord in that great day.

The questions might be asked, "Why is it necessary for our bodies to be altered? Why can we not enter heaven with our bodies as they are?" The answer is that our present bodies are designed for life in this present world. Adam's body was "earthy" (1 Cor. 15:47), and ours are as well. Adam was made "a living soul" (1 Cor. 15:45). The need for an alteration in our bodies arises from the fact that "flesh and blood cannot inherit the kingdom of God" (1 Cor. 15:50). To be fit for life in heaven, the bodies we have now must undergo a change.

The needed change to our bodies will result in this earthly body being altered into a heavenly body

(1 Cor. 15:48). Daniel informs us of this in his prophecy when he tells us from the mouth of God that "they that be wise shall shine as the brightness of the firmament; and…as the stars for ever and ever" (Dan. 12:3). Similarly, the Lord Jesus Christ declares, "Then shall the righteous shine forth as the sun in the kingdom of their Father" (Matt. 13:43). Our present bodies are patterned after the body of the first Adam; but our future bodies will be patterned after the body of Christ, the last Adam (1 Cor. 15:45–47). In this world we have a natural body, but in glory we will have a spiritual body (1 Cor. 15:46).

Obvious questions arise in our minds as we consider the implications of this mystery. What kinds of changes will our bodies undergo? What will be the resemblance of our present body to the ones we will have as believers in the resurrection? There are aspects of such questions that God has not revealed to us. But what we do know is very wonderful and lifts our hearts up in adoration of God for His great goodness.

Our present body is related to our future body in the same way as the seed is to the mature plant. Our earthly body is sown into the earth as a seed is sown, but what rises at last is greater and more wonderful (1 Cor. 15:37–38). As to the changes that will take place in our bodies at the resurrection, we learn about several significant changes from the apostle Paul. First, we learn that the body is "sown [buried at death] in corruption; it is raised in incorruption" (1 Cor. 15:42). That is to say, the resurrection body

will be incapable of deterioration or loss of its perfection. It will be beyond the possibility of sinning
or of diminishing in brightness. A second aspect of
the change is this: "It is sown in dishonor; it is raised
in glory" (1 Cor. 15:43). At its burial the body is in a
shameful state, but it will be glorious when it rises
from the grave at last. A third alteration is this: "It
is sown in weakness; it is raised in power" (1 Cor.
15:43). The corpse has no energy to do anything. But
the resurrected body will have the energy to rise to
meet the Lord in the air and to praise God eternally.
Indeed, the resurrected body will be fitted perfectly
to glorify God and to enjoy Him forever. Finally, a
fourth improvement will be this: "It is sown a natural body; it is raised a spiritual body" (1 Cor. 15:44).
By this expression "spiritual body," Paul intends us
to understand that the resurrected body will be perfectly and in every possible respect suited to eternal
life in heaven just as the earthly body that we now
have is suited to life on this earth.

In telling us of these alterations to our body at the
last day, the apostle Paul makes clear that the body
we now have and the body we will have in heaven
is one and the same. The caterpillar and the butter-
fly are the same creature, but at different stages of
development. So it is with our present body and our
future body—both have the same identity. But the
appearance and God-given powers of our bodies will
be far higher and greater when, in God's mercy, we
rise at the last day.

Will there be degrees of reward in heaven? Yes, certainly. Some will be higher than others. This seems to be indicated by the language of Paul in 1 Corinthians 15: "There is one glory of the sun, and another glory of the moon, and another glory of the stars: for one star differeth from another star in glory" (1 Cor. 15:41). Without a doubt, Christ's parable of the pounds teaches that there will be degrees of reward in heaven. Some will receive a greater reward than others. In the words of the parable, some will receive "ten cities," some "five cities," and so on (Luke 19:17, 19).

The great change that will occur to our bodies will happen in an instant. Paul's famous description is, "in a moment, in the twinkling of an eye." One moment the bodies of those who are dead and who belong to Christ will be dust; the next moment they will be living, animated, and bright as the angels of God.

This mystery of the New Testament should fill Christians with comfort and hope. We can say with Paul: "O death, where is thy sting? O grave, where is thy victory?" (1 Cor. 15:55). The true Christian will get the victory over death and the grave at last. Therefore we should seek to live wholly for God in this life and endeavor to "lay up for [ourselves] treasures in heaven" (Matt. 6:20).

But is all this true also for the unbeliever? Alas, no! The wicked will rise from the grave "to shame and everlasting contempt" (Dan. 12:2). The unbeliever should therefore repent and come to faith in Christ. God is ready to forgive all who do.

14

When All Mysteries
Are Finished

*For now we see through a glass, darkly; but
then face to face: now I know in part; but then
shall I know even as also I am known.*

—1 CORINTHIANS 13:12

God's many mysteries are only for this life. In heaven
God's people will finally see all things plainly. Mysteries that we see only in part now will be explained
fully in heaven. Doctrines that we see in this life only
very imperfectly will be clear as day in glory.

This promise of mysteries being revealed is
recorded for us in Scripture so that we might long to
be at home with Christ, when all that now perplexes
us will be explained and made clear. In this life we
are being taught to live and walk by faith. But the
moment the believer leaves this life and enters into
heaven, he will live thereafter by sight. Even our
knowledge of Christ Himself is, in this life, very limited. The "glass" (1 Cor. 13:12) in which we see Him
is the Bible, which is infallible and fully sufficient for
God's people in this present world. But the Bible itself

is a "light that shineth in a dark place, until the day dawn" (2 Peter 1:19). The Bible is perfectly sufficient for this life. But much more is to be revealed to us in the life of glory. Here we see Christ "showing himself through the lattice" (Song 2:9). But in heaven we will see Him in His transcendent glory. Then no mystery will obscure the radiance of His person or His love for all believers. God keeps the best wine until the end.

The believer enjoys many blessings out of God's hand here and now in this life, but the blessings reserved in heaven for all who trust in Christ will be far better. "The day of death" for every Christian will be better than "the day of one's birth" (Eccl. 7:1). To be with Christ will be far better than to look forward to being with Him, which is what we do now. To enjoy His love in heaven's fullness will be far better than to taste of it modestly in this life. To see Him on His throne will be far better than to get a glimpse of Him, as here and now we sometimes do through the means of grace: the Word, the sacraments, prayer, and godly fellowship.

The end of the journey will, for the believer, be better by far than the journey itself was. Here, as we travel through a desert land toward the city of Zion, we are in the midst of enemies seen and unseen. We often feel this world to be a hostile place. We say in our soul, "This is not [our] rest...it is polluted" (Micah 2:10). God has made us for Himself, and we cannot, if we are His children, feel satisfied until we have Him in full view. This, at the journey's end, we will have. "Thine eyes shall see the king in his beauty," and we "shall behold the land that is very far off" (Isa. 33:17).

Childhood is good, but maturity is better. In this life we are but children compared to what we will be in glory. Here in this world, as God's people, we speak as a child, understand as a child, and think as a child (1 Cor. 13:11). But in heaven with the Lord, when we become "men," we will "put away childish things" (1 Cor. 13:11). Every mystery will then, in the immediate presence of the great God who is our Father, be unraveled and explained. Much of our present knowledge is, as it were, "in proverbs" (John 16:25). But our Lord tells us this: "The time cometh, when I shall no more speak unto you in proverbs, but I shall show you plainly of the Father" (John 16:25). No doubt these words of our Lord have a reference to the clearer light given when the time of the New Testament would come. The words are surely also relevant to the time when we shall know even as also we are known (1 Cor. 13:12).

As the wedding day itself is better than the rehearsal, so it will be for all God's dear children. The consummation of our union and communion with the blessed Lord Himself will be far better than our most heartwarming experiences of His love here below. All true saints will then taste a measure of Christ's love for them at the wedding feast of the Lamb, which will far surpass all earthly delights. It will be the day when all saints will be ravished with "the love of Christ, which passeth knowledge" (Eph. 3:19). It will be the day when they experience what it means to be "filled with all the fulness of God" (Eph. 3:19).

As seeing is better than believing, and as enjoying is better than hoping, so will the immediate presence of Christ in all His glory be better than all books, sermons, and lectures that God has kindly given us here in this life of shadows and mysteries. As laughter and joy are better than weeping and sorrow, so will heaven be better than earth. In heaven, "God shall wipe away all tears from their eyes" (Rev. 21:4). There will at last be abundant cause for rejoicing. All sin will then be shut out of the new heavens and new earth forever. All God's children will be now gathered together out of all tongues and nations, out of all ages and generations, out of all trials, prisons, persecutions, and temptations.

The church of Christ, the "new Jerusalem" (Rev. 21:2), will be made perfectly blessed in the glorious presence of the triune God. The church herself will then have "the glory of God" (Rev. 21:11). The righteous will then "shine as the brightness of the firmament; and... as the stars for ever and ever" (Dan. 12:3).

Not only will there then be no dark mysteries; there will be no more need of created luminaries for God's children: "The sun shall be no more thy light by day; neither for brightness shall the moon give light unto thee" (Isa. 60:19). Instead of material sources of light, made to serve us here in this present life for a season, in glory there will be a source of vastly brighter light: "The LORD shall be unto thee an everlasting light, and thy God thy glory" (Isa. 60:19). With such an intense outpouring of divine light there could be no more room for any shadows, mysteries, or a lack of full assurance in all believers.

The heaven that awaits believers is a world of absolute and complete perfection. There, God will be perfectly glorified by all His people. There, God the Trinity will be perfectly loved by the entire heavenly host. All the promises of Scripture to believers will be fully and forever made good. All prophecies of God that we now read in Scripture will prove to have been inspired, infallible, and most sure. Not a syllable of all that God has said to us will fail to be carried out at last.

Every attribute of God will be perfectly glorified. His love, justice, and wisdom will be seen by all in heaven to have supervised creation, providence, and the judgment day with meticulous perfection and consummate righteousness.

All the eternal and secret decrees of God, made by Him before the world began, will then appear clearly to be fulfilled at last to absolute and total perfection. Not one of His elect will be lost, left behind, or overlooked by the sovereign Jehovah. Each of His redeemed children will then be able to testify to the reality in his or her own experience of God's saving and converting grace. They will all put their amen to the affirmation of Christ: "Ye have not chosen me, but I have chosen you" (John 15:16). In glory it will be God's free grace, not man's free will, that will be eternally praised and admired.

Thanks be to God for the mysteries of Scripture that light up our path to the land of glory that lies ahead. Blessed be the triune God who has shown us by the Bible how unworthy sinners may get safely to heaven by faith in Christ!